I SPY
with my little eye...

VEHICLES

Remember: Just like real I SPY GAME,

letters are not in alphabetical order.

I spy with my little eye something beginning with...

T

is for

TAXI

I spy with my little eye something beginning with...

D is for

DUMP TRUCK

I spy with my little eye something beginning with...

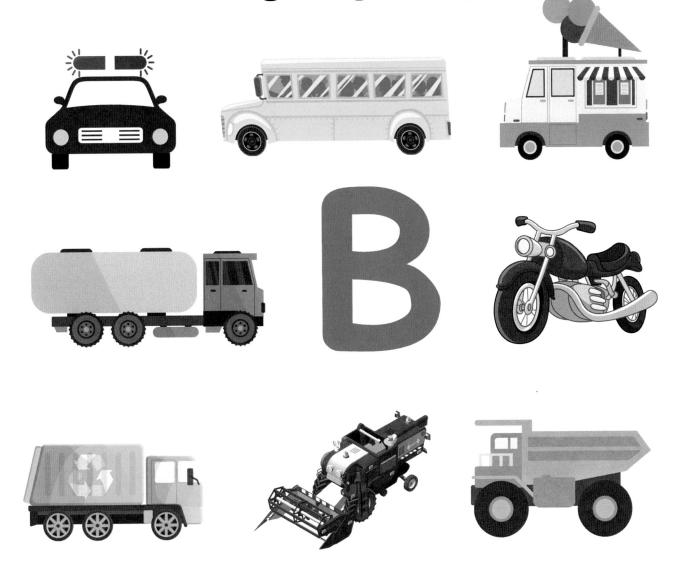

B is for

BUS

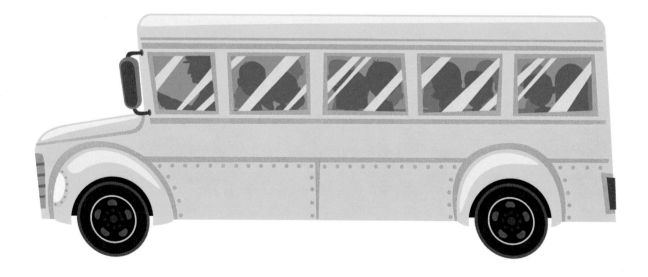

I spy with my little eye something beginning with...

H is for

HARVESTER

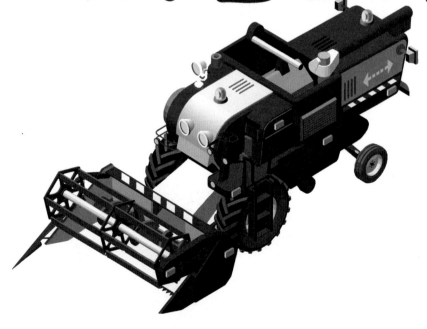

I spy with my little eye something beginning with...

E is for

EXCAVATOR

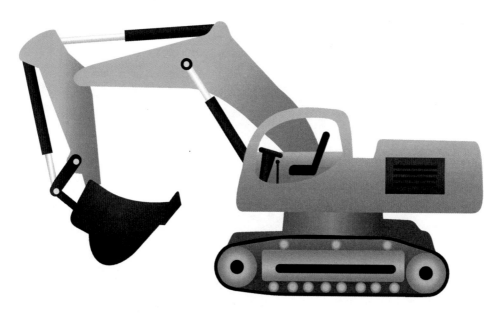

I spy with my little eye something beginning with...

P is for

POLICE CAR

I spy with my little eye something beginning with...

A is for

AMBULANCE

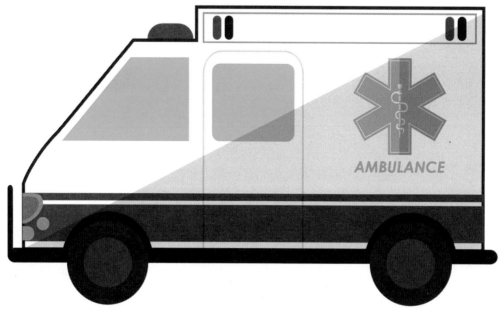

I spy with my little eye something beginning with...

I is for

ICE CREAM CAR

I spy with my little eye something beginning with...

M is for
MINING TRUCK

I spy with my little eye something beginning with...

F is for

FORK LIFT

I spy with my little eye something beginning with...

C is for

CRANE CAR

I spy with my little eye something beginning with...

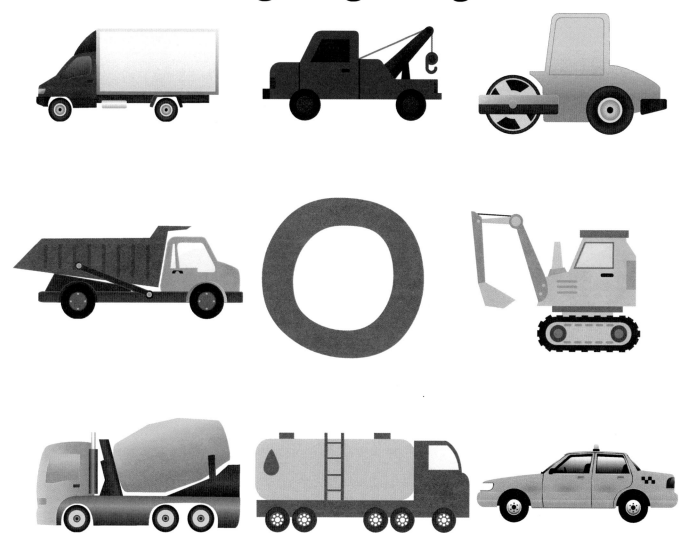

O is for

OIL TANKER CAR

I spy with my little eye something beginning with...

V is for

VAN

I spy with my little eye something beginning with...

R is for

ROAD ROLLER

I spy with my little eye something beginning with...

W is for

WHEEL LOADER

I spy with my little eye something beginning with...

G is for

GARBAGE CAR

See our other products

Made in the USA
Monee, IL
28 September 2021